A Wilkes-Barre Christmas Story

A wonderful town makes Christmas all the better

> Wilkes-Barre, PA may not be Bedford Falls but it is a great place to lead a wonderful life. It may not be Mayberry, but it is my hometown.
>
> Wilkes-Barre is the setting of this light-hearted story of a young Wilkes-Barre boy with a 26" bike. The boy had a burning desire to have a train set to go around the family Christmas tree each year.
>
> This story is true and it really did happen in Wilkes-Barre, PA., a real city. It takes the reader on a journey using a 26" 1950's style homemade bicycle starting from when the boy was five years old and it ends when he is nine. Either a miracle happens or the Christmas Spirit or Santa or all three bring forth one of the happiest and most amazing moments that any child can experience in a lifetime.
>
> Not all stories – even Christmas stories end well. This incredible story will not disappoint any reader once you mount the 26" bike right next to the young boy as he goes through the preparations and the work efforts and adventures within this story. The ending is outstanding. If it were not true, it would still make a great Christmas story. Since it is true, it makes it even more special, especially for me. I am the boy in the story. Thank you for reading it... It could only happen in a great town such as Wilkes-Barre, PA

BRIAN W. KELLY

Merry Christmas

Copyright © Nov 2017, Brian W. Kelly Publisher: Brian P. Kelly
Title: A Wilkes-Barre Christmas Story Author: Brian W. Kelly

All rights reserved: No part of this book may be reproduced or transmitted in any form, or by any means, electronic or mechanical, including photocopying, recording, scanning, faxing, or by any information storage and retrieval system, without permission from the publisher, LETS GO PUBLISH, in writing.

Disclaimer: Though judicious care was taken throughout the writing and the publication of this work that the information contained herein is accurate, there is no expressed or implied warranty that all information in this book is 100% correct. Therefore, neither LETS GO PUBLISH, nor the author accepts liability for any use of this work.

Trademarks: A number of products and names referenced in this book are trade names and trademarks of their respective companies.

Referenced Material: *Standard Disclaimer:* The information in this book has been obtained through personal and third party observations, interviews, and copious research. Where unique information has been provided or extracted from other sources, those sources are acknowledged within the text of the book itself or at the end of the chapter in the Sources Section. Thus, there are no formal footnotes nor is there a bibliography section. Any picture that does not have a source was taken from various sites on the Internet with no credit attached. If resource owners would like credit in the next printing, please email publisher.

Published by: LETS GO PUBLISH!
Publisher Brian P. Kelly
Email: info@letsgopublish.com
Web site www.letsgopublish.com

Library of Congress Copyright Information Pending
Book Cover Design by Brian W. Kelly
Editor—Brian P. Kelly

ISBN Information: The International Standard Book Number (ISBN) is a unique machine-readable identification number, which marks any book unmistakably. The ISBN is the clear standard in the book industry. 159 countries and territories are officially ISBN members. The Official ISBN For this book is on the outside cover:

ISBN 978-1-947402-16-4

The price for this work is: $11.95 USD

10   9   8   7   6   5   4   3   2   1

Release Date: November 2017

Publisher's Note: *Please check out www.letsgopublish.com for BK books & to read the latest version of my heartfelt acknowledgments updated for this book. Click the bottom item of the Main menu on the site!*

Merry Christmas

My name is:

_____

Dedication

Special Thanks Are Extended:

To My Brothers

And Sisters,

Ed, Nancy Flannery, Mary Daniels & Joe

Plus

My Children, Brian, Michael & Katie

Plus
My best buddies Dennis and Barbara Grimes & Gerry Rodski and Joyce Heck.

You all have been bugging me for years to write a book such as this.

Thank you all, including Wily Ky Eyely for being so kind!

Preface

Wilkes-Barre, PA may not be Bedford Falls but it is a great place to lead a wonderful life. It may not be Mayberry, but it is my hometown.

Wilkes-Barre is the setting of this light-hearted story of a young Wilkes-Barre boy with a 26" bike, who had a burning desire to have a train set to go around the family Christmas tree each year.

This book is a remake of a book that I wrote a year ago and had titled Four Dollars and Sixty-Two-Cents. After reading the book again to make the updates, I realized that as much as this book is about me as a little kid, thrilled to be alive in Wilkes-Barre, it is as much about Wilkes-Barre itself as I remember the City.

And, so in this, the second repackaging of this story this year, I decided to celebrate Wilkes-Barre, PA where the story takes place. I had already corrected the original book and released it with a different title: *A Boy, a Bike, A Train, & A Christmas Miracle*. After thinking about this project, having updated the original book, I realized that from the beginning, I had really written a Wilkes-Barre Christmas Story. And, it was only when I wrote this paragraph just five minutes ago, that I figured out what to call this book:

A Wilkes-Barre Christmas Story.

A Wilkes-Barre Christmas Story is a perfect title as it is exactly what this book is about–a heartwarming apologue that is filled with the Christmas spirit. I then thought about a sub-title for the book so I could say something nice about my hometown. It came out as

A wonderful town makes Christmas all the better.

This story is true and it really did happen in Wilkes-Barre, PA., of which I can attest is a real city, just 16 miles south of Scranton, the hometown of The Office.

It takes the reader on a journey using a 26" 1950's style homemade bicycle starting from when the boy was five years old and it ends when he is nine. Either a miracle happens or the Christmas Spirit or Santa or all three bring forth one of the happiest and most amazing moments that any child can hope to experience in a lifetime.

Not all stories – even Christmas stories end well. This incredible true story will not disappoint any reader once you mount the 26" bike right next to the young boy as he goes through the preparations and the work efforts and adventures within this story. The ending is outstanding. If it were not true, it would make a great Christmas fable. Since it is true, it makes it even more special, especially for me. I am the boy in the story. Thank you for reading it… It could only happen in a great town such as Wilkes-Barre, PA

Table of Contents

Chapter 1 Nothing Like a Kid And a 26" Bike 1
Chapter 2 Built from Junkyard Parts 11
Chapter 3 A One-Of-A-Kind Bike 23
Chapter 4 More about My First 26" Bike 33
Chapter 5 A 26" Bike Can Take a Kid Anywhere! 37
Chapter 6 A Neighborhood Bike 45
Chapter 7 Change for a Nickel? 57
Chapter 8 We Had Two 5 & 10c Stores in Wilkes-Barre 63
Chapter 9 How Could a Kid Not Want an Electric Train? .. 69
Chapter 10 I Still Love Trains 77
Chapter 11 Sometimes Dreams Do Come True 83
Chapter 12 It Felt Different This Time 97
Chapter 13 Getting the New Train Set Home to Work 109
Other books by Brian Kelly: (amazon.com, and Kindle) 122

Chapter 1 Nothing In The World Like a Kid And a 26" Bike

The setting for *A Wilkes-Barre Christmas Story,* is my hometown, Wilkes-Barre, PA. As I noted in the Preface of this book, my hometown may not be Bedford Falls but it was a great place to lead my wonderful life. It may not be Mayberry, but it was my hometown, which gave me all I needed as I grew up.

And, folks, Wilkes-Barre to those who have lived here at one time or another, is pronounced as Wilkes-Berry and that means that it rhymes with Mayberry. And that means we can sing their song without melody changes.

Everybody has a soft spot for their own hometown, and hearing that wonderful song

Mayberry sung on the ME TV's Andy Griffith Show's TV advertisements is enough to bring a yearning for your hometown and my hometown right to our hearts.

So, let us begin this story about a young Wilkes-Barre boy, who loved Christmas by singing Earle Hagen's now famous "My Hometown."

Clear out the pipes and let's give it a go along with Keevy Hazelton, Aunt Bee Taylor and Clara Edwards. Why Not?

Get ready. Here are the Words for the sing-along:

```
My hometown is the greatest place I know
Where the neighbors I find are gentle and kind
And the living easy and slow


My hometown is the only place to be
Here the worries are small & the kids grow tall
And strong and healthy and free

It's my hometown, my hometown

Wilkesberry, Wilkesberry
```

OK, Hollywood would say Mayberry but around Northeastern PA, we would enjoy saying in our special twang, Wilkesberry.

Yes, kids and older folks, I was born back in the glory days of Wilkes-Barre, Pennsylvania. I always remember my home and my hometown being quite special as I was growing up. I loved the City and I loved where I lived.

By the way, I lived right next door to a silk mill that operated twenty-four hours a day. My brothers and sisters and I wonder today why we do not hear as well as we should.

All night long, especially with windows wide open in the summer to get some cool air, we were treated to the same old song every night.

We never gave it a name but the song went like this: *"Whoosh Whoosh Eee Eee Whoosh Whoosh"* Each line of the song was the same It was the mill machines working overtime.

Here is a little snoop inside the mill which has now morphed into a nice winery at 373 High Street. My address was 363 High Street, Wilkes-Barre, Pennsylvania

Our neighborhood was unique, I would say. Besides the huge mill, there were three stores on our little block and a tavern—my cousin Arlene's place.

Right across the street from Arlene's was the big mile-deep coal car elevator for the South Wilke-Barre Coal Colliery. Miners often enjoyed wetting their whistles at my cousin Arlene's place both before and after their work shifts.

In fact, as I recall, there was a tavern on every block on the streets by our neighborhood. On some blocks, there were even two. The miners never had to travel far for a cool one.

It seems that as soon as I could walk, I could ride a bike. I mean a big 26" bike. I had learned to ride a two-wheeler on a 16-inch bike on Brown

Street—just one block up from High Street where I was born and lived.

My cousin Rich Knaus, who I loved like a brother, had a 16-inch bike with training wheels before we were even five years old.

We rode it on the sidewalk by his house on Brown Street. When his dad, Hank Fibick, took off the training wheels, both of us could ride his bike. It was great! We grew up fast with two wheels.

It was not much more than a year later that I was hoping to get a bike of my own. I was five or six years old. I am not kidding.

My dad bought my first bike for me for a dollar. I knew my father had no dimes to spare so this was unexpected but much appreciated.

Karly Blaine made the bike out of stuff he had gotten at George Solomon Sr.'s Junk Yard on Parrish Street. It was less than a block and a half from home.

My buddy George Elias who grew up with me on High Street said this about Karly Blaine:

"Karly Blaine manufactured so many bikes, he should have opened a factory."

Two great junk yards were little more than a block away

Alexander's Junkyard was on Gould Lane right off Blackman Street. Solomon's Junk Yard was on Parrish Street.

Alexander himself was the dad of a great guy whom the young ladies in our new neighborhood, Jeannie Elin & Carol Stett call "Lar Lar." Some say their boyfriends, John and Joe never got jealous. Alexander's junk yard on Gould Lane, was just ½ block from Parrish Street.

The backs of Solomon's and Alexander's touched. Alexander's was almost as close to my house as Solomon's junk yard but Solomon's place was much bigger or so it seemed as a child.

The Silk Mill parking lot, which was behind my house on High Street also touched part of Alexander's and part of Solomon's. But, the fences were high enough to keep us out. They had barbed wire at the top so we would go under them to get into the Mill Yard to play ball.

We were also able to sneak in the front driveway of Solomon's Junkyard whenever we needed used bike parts.

More importantly to me, Solomon's took in a lot of bikes, bike frames, fenders, chain guards, forks, and other bike parts.

They were mixed in with metal appliances, car frames, car rims, and other metal objects. The great bike parts were not always easy to spot.

You can get an idea of what a pile of scrap looked like in the picture on the next page. I could not find Solomon's or Alexander's in any archives because both "yards" went out of business more than fifty years ago.

Picture of General Junk Yard with Few Bike Parts

You can see from the picture above why the junkyard workers were concerned when we climbed the piles at Solomon's looking for bike treasures.

The men who worked at the junkyard just threw the bikes up on what had to be a fifteen-foot-high junk pile. We had no problem climbing the pile after the junk settled.

The bikes did not last long. Along with small cars and car parts, they were crushed into two-foot by two-foot metal bricks. After that, the junk yard shipped these huge metal bricks someplace to recycle the metal.

My friends and I climbed those piles like they were a mountain of free toys and we often found some great bike parts and other great stuff. We knew that we had to get there for new treasures before the stuff was crushed.

It was not easy to find bike gear though. It was also a little scary when they were running the metal crusher that was fed by a huge scrap magnet.

The scrap metal magnet filled the crusher

The magnet was somewhat quiet when in use. Its noise mixed in with the overall eerie junkyard sound. I recall no junkyard dogs protecting the place and if there were, this story never could have been told. I can't recall a bark.

But when they turned the baler on to crush the metal—scary! That was a frightful sound.

I could not find a good picture of an old scrap metal baler so I found a picture of this huge claw getting ready to pick up a car. This would drop the car into the baler and the big bales were then made as the car disappeared.

Some places stored their huge scrap bales like bricks, neat as a pin. Others, such as Solomon's, put them wherever they could find room in the yard. When stacked, the metal bales looked pretty scary–like this:

Chapter 2 Built from Junkyard Parts

Bicycle Tree Ornament

When we were not taking things from the junkyard, we brought things in to receive payment. We never brought anything we had taken in for payment. We brought metal, paper, and rags to both the junkyards to get paid. We got paid but it was never really much, but it was always enough.

Where else, but in Wilkes-Barre PA would there be entrepreneurial opportunities for all regardless of age. Too young was actually OK and I loved that it was.

When I was five years old, I had a junk route in which every Saturday, I would knock on neighbor's doors as far as four blocks away. They would save me papers and rags.

Typically, I would get ½ cent per pound for old newspapers and magazines and 2 cents per pound for rags as long as the rags were clean. On a typical Saturday, I would make between 30 cents and 50 cents for the day. I thought that was great.

I once had a radio flyer wagon that looked like the one below but it did not last long. It was rusty and hard to pull. I put two cardboard boxes in it and put the papers in the boxes. It did not hold much.

There was a well-endowed Salvation Army on the other end of High Street by Hazle, about five blocks away from our home. They sold big baby carriages there for 10 cents apiece. Whenever I went there, they had about five or ten of these carriages lined up. They were all in great shape for expecting moms, available for a dime each. I stopped using wagons as the carriages were easier.

The baby carriages were much easier to push than the Radio Flier wagons and each carriage fitted two columns of newspapers, stacked neatly side by side. It was like the carriages were made for the small-hauling scrap newspaper business.

Even though the price at the two junkyards was supposed to be the same, Alexander's always gave a better price than Solomon's for a bunch of rags, if they were clean. But, Alexander did not like to receive small amounts of newspapers so I would take them to Solomon's.

Mr. Sam Alexander was a great guy, as was Mr. George Solomon Sr. and Mike Solomon, his son. I admit I was afraid of them all—especially when they yelled at me to get off the big junk piles when I was hunting for bike parts. When we found stuff, they never let us pay for anything we took.

The Solomon Junk Yard workers did not care what kids like Karly Blaine and I took from the yard, or so it seemed.

What they could not tolerate, however, was kids on the top of the dangerous junk piles looking for great stuff. We did not think we were thieves like the guy in the picture below.

Suspected stolen bike chop shops

(Photo: Mike Skeels)

We took the risk because the reward was so great. We were all unbreakable little men then; but the Solomon people did not know it.

So, they would give us the chase when they saw us on top of the big piles looking for past bicycle treasures.

If we had a good day finding stuff, and we were leaving with some bounty, such as a rim or a shock absorbing bike fork, a sprocket, or a glistening handlebar, the men at Solomon's would pretend they did not see us.

Perhaps they just hoped we would leave quickly.

They turned their eyes to enable our escape with our loot, but they did not like to see us ten or fifteen feet up high on those junk piles—no matter how much they seemed to like kids like us.

One day, Karly Blaine completed the biggest deed of anybody ever in my young life. He was several years older than me.

He had had a successful mission at Solomon's and he amassed all the parts he needed to make a "new" homemade 26" bike.

I never saw him up there on the piles when I was there, but I knew he did not get the stuff out of thin air.

The bike that Karly built had a beat-up frame that had been painted with cheap 5c & 10c store paint several times. It might have even been house paint.

Looking at an inexact replica below, may I suggest that if we took off the back carrier of this mud-encrusted bike and the chain guard and if we added a fat seat, gave it a good washing, and added some old blue house paint, the bike below could quickly look a lot like the bike Karly Blaine made for me. Except his bike had big fat tires and they were inflated and they held air. :

That's how tough looking the bike remnants of the 1950's looked when they were captured. The Karly bike that my dad bought had a not-so-shiny, partly rusty, handle bar, with no fenders, and no chain guard.

The Karly bike not only had rims; it had two tube tires filled with air. They were almost bald but the tubes held air and did not leak.

The foot breaks even worked. They were called "New Departure" style brakes. When you peddled backwards, the wheel stops and the bike skids. The best thing of all was that the Karly bike itself was in working order and it was ready to be ridden. Karly did it. He made it from old junkyard parts.

In putting this book together, I looked for old pictures of me and my trusty bike but I came up empty. I did find some pictures of the kind of bikes available from junkyards back then.

But no picture that I examined captured the full rag-tag look of the 26" bike Karly Blaine had made for me. My bike was built with a very old Roadmaster frame with fat tires. Here is a much nicer narrow-tire version of the bike I once called my own:

Since I am showing bike pictures, please let me get out of sequence on my timeline for a minute. I'll be back to finish this up right away.

As I got older, I got good at recognizing the good old bikes from the bad old bikes.

Often those bikes that were painted many, many, times had their emblems painted over and it was tough to tell the good styles and models from the bad. But I could usually tell.

When I found a frame for a Roadmaster or a Schwinn, at the junkyard, it was always a grand day. In other words, it was a real treat.

Here are a few photos that show these types of bikes looking new in 1952 and in 1955. Notice the fat tires.

If you take all the bells and whistles and fancy parts off this guy, my big 26 "bike was a lot more like the Roadmaster than the new Schwinn which is shown on the next page:

Boys 26-inch Model F14

The bike above is from a 1955 catalog. It is a Schwinn, which is still a big name in bikes. The tires on the Schwinn are way too narrow compared to my 26" beauty. The frame of my thick-tire bike of course was painted by the same type of paint as one would use to paint a house. Few people who I know could have afforded real bike paint.

Chapter 3 A One-Of-A-Kind Bike

I have not yet returned to finish the Karly Blaine Wilkes-Barre Bike Story. One more diversion, please.

I had been showing bike pictures in the prior chapter and so this chapter is sort of out of chronological sequence. I want you to know that the best bike I ever had was given to me a few years later than my first bike made by Karly Blaine.

It was given to me by Officer Billy Walters of the PA State Police. My buddies Mark George, from Avoca, PA, and Danny Olejniak from Sugarnotch, PA, both retired State Police Officers, who I respect implicitly, would have really liked Billy Walters

Billy was my father's high school friend who had become a PA State Policeman and then a beat COP in Philadelphia. He was a great man and of course I called him Mr. Walters.

Billy married later in life and he had no children. He married a cousin of my cousin Kathleen Kelly McKeown, who had married my cousin Joseph McKeown, Jr. There was a connection with the great Spinning Wheel in Wilkes-Barre but I do not recall exactly what it was.

Billy Walters loved coming to our house around Christmas before those days. Our home was always loaded with kids. Around the holidays.

We had the five Kelly kids, my brothers and sisters, plus our cousin Rich Knaus, and other kids from the visiting out-of-town relatives.

Though we had lots of kids in the house, we had only three bedrooms, which were used by adult out-of-towners mostly from New Jersey so the floors were loaded at night with bedding and kids' bodies.

When he was visiting us one Christmas, Mr. Walters, a City Cop in Philadelphia, who never came with hands empty kept his gift record clean.

In his area of work, he got to stop at a lot of great places such as a Whitman's Candy House, who appreciated his great service.

I am not sure if it was Whitman's the company or a store that sold Whitman's Chocolates. As a policeman, the Whitman's people appreciated Mr. Walters for keeping thieves away and keeping them safe.

Mr. Walters or Billy, as my dad called him. never came to our home empty handed. His signature gift was an unmarked five-pound box of Whitman's Sampler Chocolates. If it were marked, it would look like this:

To this day, I cannot recall seeing a box of candy quite so large. There was something on the bottom of the box that said it was Whitman's Sampler or Miniatures, but you would never have known it.

Every Christmas until he got married, Billy Walters visited my father at Christmas time. Sometimes we would go to his mother's home during the Christmas Season. My dad worked at Stebmaier's but the drank Kaers. He would normally complain about the beer but with Billy, everything was OK. Billy's mom was named Pearl.

I remember she had a Chinese Gong. It sounded really neat like one of the great Far Eastern movies. All you had to do was give it a whack with the striker or mallet and everybody in the house would notice.

The striker is shown on the bottom left

The stick in the picture that looks like a huge Q-tip is the gong's drumstick! Yes, whenever I was there I found the striker and whacked the gong until I made a pest of myself.

Out of nowhere a really big gift for a kid

One day, when Mr. Walters was visiting our Wilkes-Barre home, he told my grandmother that he had a paratrooper bike for me just like the kind they used in the War. I did not know what to expect. Once I knew it was coming, it seemed like forever waiting and I had grown skeptical.

But one day, Billy did come with the bike. I thanked him profusely and I made sure that he knew that I loved what he had done.

Big Problem with The New Bike

It sure needed a washing from being stored for years. It did not look new at all. As soon as I had a chance, I gave it that washing. After the wash, it was a dark dull red but there was still one big thing wrong.

Even the bike Karly Blaine had made was a boy's-bike with the bars across the top and a third bar down to the sprocket.

This "paratrooper" bike had just one bar. It was from the handle bars down to the sprocket. Here is a classic Roadmaster girl's bike:

I started to think the paratroopers bike had to be for a lady paratrooper because it had girl's bike characteristics.

That would not do. I was already thinking about how I could get rid of it. It bothered me that it seemed like a girl's bike.

Unlike the two bars from the front to the sprocket on a girl's bike, this bike had a big thick bar from the front to the sprocket. It was twice as thick as any bike frame I had ever seen.

But I could not get it out of my head that it looked like a girl's bike

It had a knob on the bar near the sprocket that I could not figure out. I could not move it. I was so curious that I got some *Liquid Wrench* as there was no WD-40 at home at hand. Before long, I could turn the knob.

When I got it all the way turned the bike fell apart. I thought I had broken it. My grandmother called Billy Walters. He told her about the magic that was part of every paratrooper bike.

So that the paratroopers could jump from airplanes during the war with their bicycles in their arms or attached to their bodies, the army created this bike and built it specially.

It could be split in half and could be reattached in less than a minute. I took the information from my Grand Mom and I re-attached the two pieces Wow! Not only was this not a girl's bike; it was a man's bike.

It was a one-of-a-kind 26" bike. Was I lucky guy! I felt guilty about my girl's bike thoughts but I got over it. It gave a smooth ride—much better than any bike I ever rode.

It did not matter to me as much that it was the most solid bike I had ever seen. Better than that, it was representative of the World War that America had just won ten years earlier. The guys and the girls on my street and everybody I ever met were impressed. I had one heck of a story to tell about that bike.

Nobody thought it was a girl's bike even before I told them the story. I wish I had the picture shown below to show how the bike was used during the war. In this case, a picture would be worth a thousand words. Here it is:

Now that we have talked about all the choices of bicycles that I had during the youngest parts of my life, it is time for us to finish the Karly Blaine bike story of my first bicycle. Karly lived right across the street from our house on High St.

Thank you for letting me talk about all these bikes before we move on to the rest of this story.

Back to My First Bike

Looking back on my first bike, I cannot believe that my extremely cautious dad had paid the dollar to get me the bike of my dreams.

I was thrilled. He never saw the bike until I was on it the next day and I rode it up to our curb at 363 High Street in Wilkes-Barre, PA.

From the Karly Blaine bike to a paratrooper bike in just a few years was something I never would have believed when I had my first bicycle.

Chapter 4 More about the Karly Blaine Bike (My First 26" Bike)

My street, High Street, as a number of streets in Wilkes-Barre, was made of small stones and tar/oil. It was not like the smooth asphalt streets of today.

The street department would refresh our street every few years. They would start by getting all the cars off the street. They would then pour hot oil on the street so it looked slick black.

They did this about every other summer. It refreshed the look and got rid of the pot holes. They patched the potholes before lathering the street with oil/tar. There were no asphalt machines required.

After the oil pour, they would put fresh tiny light red stones on the street and the stones would cover up the oil.

Eventually, cars would ride over the surface and it would take on a look somewhat like asphalt streets of today but never quite as smooth. The stones and the oil would become a solid road.

The road was never perfect but it was good enough. High Street always tapered down to our sidewalk as most of the stones stayed on the crest of the road.

The taper that ended at the gutter on High Street was about six inches lower than the curb. So, our curbs were about six inches high or better and very ready to support a kid's foot from a 26" bike.

You probably already can figure out that there was one problem with my first 26" bike, when I was between five and six years old. I was way too small to get on it.

Karly Blaine put me on the bike nonetheless the first day and I rode it down High Street to Parrish and back fine though my feet barely made it to the petals.

I knew he would not be there every time for me so I figured out what to do.

I stopped by the big 6-inch curb in front of my house and put my foot down and I was able to get off.

For about six months until I got taller, I used those high curbs to mount and dismount my 26" bicycle. I was so proud and so thankful.

It never seemed to matter to anybody, nor to me that I needed every inch to mount the bike.

And of course, before I got a little bigger, it was always tough getting more than my toes on the petals once on my way.

It sure was an adventure and a very successful one. For a year or so, I did not ride my bike more than a block from the house. When I was able to finally put more than my toes on the petals, my exploring days were just beginning.

Chapter 5 A 26" Bike Can Take a Kid Anywhere!

Off to see the world!

Once mounted on my mean fender-less machine, I was a bike monster from then on. I often think back about how Karly got the bike parts. We never stole anything from anybody.

To be honest, when we took things from the junkyard, we never once thought it was stealing. I do not know why! It surely was stealing but they kind of let us do it.

Now I know it was grand theft larceny but back then none of us knew.

I am sure Karly Blaine felt the same way. It was like the junk yard was there just for us.

I eventually learned from Karly Blaine and Joey Pahler, another High Street neighborhood guy a bit older than I, how to fix the brakes and change flats on my old but trusty 26-inch bike.

Like the older guys in the neighborhood, I became a regular at Solomon's Junk Yard.

It satisfied my bicycle parts needs and it also was the only junkyard where I could bring my carriage-loads of trash newspapers for cash every weekend.

Solomon's weighed the papers and paid kids and others for recycling newspapers. Even though I received just ½ cent per pound, I would leave the junkyard with a few nickels or dimes, and sometimes, but rarely, a quarter. Each Saturday, I would make at least two trips to the junkyard.

I soon became a little businessman. My little junk route on High Street and Parrish Street on Saturdays helped me get some money to save as well as to buy pea shooters, water guns, yo-yo's, whiffle-balls, and every now and then a soda or a candy bar.

If I did not ask for the papers and rags, they would put them out for the trash every week. I am not sure if this saved them time but they liked giving me their junk.

I was a chubby kid in my early years, so I suspect those who knew me then figured I spent most of my earnings on ice cream or soda but they would be wrong.

My route took me up Parrish Street as far as the three long blocks and past the top of the hill almost to Loomis Street

I was once spooked before Loomis Street and after that I never quite made it to the fourth block at Loomis Street. Besides, the farther up the hill I went, the longer the trip was back to Solomon's Junk Yard.

A smart young businessman would not spend all day on Saturday on a junk route just to earn one more nickel.

Right past Loomis Street moving up on Parrish on the left was St. Patrick's, a beautiful and grand church where I was baptized. Back then, the Pastor of St. Patrick's was Father Hughes. Now, the Pastor is Father Kearney and the Parish has a new name—St. Andrew's.

I had been to St. Patrick's many times but never by myself. Across from St. Pat's was Hughes Street and the next block was Hazle Street, where both Huntzinger's 5 & 10c and The Hart Theatre were both located.

At the time that I had my junk route, my dad joined St. Boniface Parish because if he stayed at St. Patrick's, he would have had to pay tuition for five children. As a member of St. Boniface, tuition was free for all of my brothers and sisters and I.

Here is a picture of St. Patrick's Church and a picture of St. Boniface Church after it had closed.

St. Patrick's Church   Former St. Boniface Church

Bonanza at the Holy Grate

One day a lady half-way up Parrish Street from Brown gave me a big iron grate that had covered their hot air furnace on their living-room floor.

My baby carriage (much more efficient than a wagon back then) was not ready for heavy lifting nor was I. She and her husband helped lift the grate onto my junk hauling carriage.

The twin "baby" carriage was almost full of papers at the time so the carriage did not collapse.

The papers supported the grate. Without going any farther up the street on that trip, I headed off right away. I held the heavy carriage back on the way to the junk yard down the steep hill. I made it. And the reward was plentiful.

The Solomon junkyard chiefs were suspicious that I might have stolen the register (grate). But, of course they knew me from being there so many times before with papers and rags. They believed my story of how I had gotten the floor grate from the lady. They had to lift it off my carriage. I was still too little for the heavy stuff.

They gave me fifty cents for the grate. The wrote 50c on one slip of paper and a 10c on another. I took the slips into Solomon's Office and they paid me the 50c plus a dime for the papers.

The grate was "heavy metal" made out of cast-iron. I had never made much more than thirty or forty cents after working all day on a Saturday. It was my best day ever on my junk route for years. After cashing out, I went back up Parrish Street hill and finished my route.

My other venture as I have already confessed at the junk yard was to keep my bikes in the best of shape and looking as good as possible without needing 5 & 10c paint.

I soon learned how to be able to recognize a great bike part from Solomon's junk yard when I was up on the pile. I developed a hawk eye! I admit when I was on a parts mission, I always had a whirring of fear in my stomach.

When I was on the big scrap pile, I felt that somebody was going to yell at me at any moment and often somebody did. Hey kid! But, the rewards were substantial, and nobody seemed to care when we were on our way out with a few parts.

Chapter 6 A Neighborhood Bike

That 26" bike changed my life even though, as noted, when I first got it, my feet could hardly reach the petals. When younger, I was always able to find a high curb or a set of front porch steps so I could get on and off.

I had some crashes and they hurt parts of my body that I did not realize were there. Of course, this helped me ride my bike even better so this would rarely happen.

Equipped with my own bike transportation, eventually I began to frequent any place in Wilkes-Barre that I chose. Kids like me did not worry about bad people (predators) back then.

None of us were worried about predators. All the kids seemed a lot tougher than the types of bad people that might try to bother us.

All I had to do was mount my personal twenty-six-inch fat tired bike, and poof! I was in a different world.

As I said previously, my "new" bike had no fenders. So, it was not too pleasant riding in rain or snow. But, I managed. It was tough avoiding a big slide when it snowed. My mom and grandmother did the wash.

We lived in a great spot on a flat street that was on the side of a big Wilkes-Barre hill called the Rolling Mill Hill. Our street was not at the top of the hill but it was named High Street nonetheless.

Lots of stores were close by so I did not always have to use my bike. However, most often, I had it with me just in case.

Places within walking distance to and from our home on High Street by Blackman, included some great spots to visit with or without a bike.

One of my favorite spots was Brady's Lunch on Blackman St. It was about two full blocks from our house down Blackman Street. Brady Moses had the famous Chile for Hot Dogs long before I knew about Abe's Hot Dogs, another popular spot in Wilkes-Barre even today.

There are two Abe's Hotdogs places from different families in Wilkes-Barre. One is the original on Barney Street and the other from the other family is the original Abe's on South Main Street. People in Wilkes-Barre know the difference.

Brady's Lunch had a steamer for the buns. Brady would grab a bun from the steamer, put on the grilled dog, slather it with mustard, and add onions. Then, he would delicately add the homemade special Chile that he made every day.

I can't compare a Brady's with an Abe's today but I bet Brady's dogs would stack up well. They were the best you could get when I was a kid.

My uncle Gene McKeown lived on Brown Street, about two blocks in total from our house but they seemed to be long blocks. He and his wife, my Aunt Helen, were my cousin Rich's grandparents. They loved Brady's hot dogs and hamburgers.

Out of the blue one day when I was still thinking about a twenty-six-inch bike, Uncle Gene called.

It was the middle of the winter-cold and windy but no snow. Nobody wanted to move from their homes but my relatives were very hungry for Brady's hot dogs.

Uncle Gene, who I liked for many reasons, asked if I would come up his house to get some cash to get his order of Brady's hamburgers with Chile and onions and hot dogs with Chile and onions.

I liked Uncle Gene so much and having been trained in a Catholic home, I would have done whatever I could with no compensation.

My cousin Rich Knaus was there often as Uncle Gene and Aunt Helen were his grandparents, but he had moved back to New Jersey after the summer. I knew Uncle Gene needed me to get his order. So, of course, I said "yes."

Hot Dogs were about two for a quarter and Hamburgers were about 20 cents at the time at Brady's Lunch. Uncle Gene gave me the cash.

I walked to Brady's and gave Brady himself the order. There was more than enough to pay for the whole order. I also got some change. Then, I headed back to Brown Street with the most deliciously smelling bag of all time.

When I got back to uncle Gene's everything was still warm. He and Aunt Helen smelled the delivery bag and they could not wait to complete the transaction with me and send me on my way.

After handing over the change, I was ready to leave when they said to wait a minute and it was less than that.

They gave me a zillion dollars as a tip for going or so it seemed. They were very generous. It was far more than I would make on a Saturday on the junk route.

I hope I asked them if they meant to give me as much as they did. I no longer have any idea of how much tip I got but it was big and totally unexpected.

No matter how cold it was outside or how tired I might be playing hard on High Street, I took the call to get the hamburgs and hot dogs whenever it came in.

The love I had for Uncle Gene and the bounty I received from a simple trip to Brady's was worth my time for sure. I often got the call. I never hesitated.

I would even stop in the middle of a game if need-be to get whatever my Uncle Gene and my Aunt Helen needed from Brady's lunch. Then I would hurry back to the game.

We often played football and baseball right in the middle of High Street for hours at a time. Ricky Solomon, Steve Barrouk, Stan Fidrych, Bill Eydler, Bobby Broody, Skippy Elias, George Eget, Bobby and Billy Owens, George Elias, Bobby Stanton, and some others participated in the High Street athletics. It was a wonderful street in a wonderful city.

God was good to me indeed! A dollar or a portion of a dollar thereof never came easily to a kid from High Street. We could not afford to say "NO," to our "customers."

Peters' Ice Cream Store was on the corner of Brown & Blackman streets.

Thunsie Peters is the owner but he shares the duties with his brother and my good friend Butchie Peters, who is just a skosh older than I.

Over the years I have done odd jobs for the Peters' family. I would shovel snow in front of their stores and when I was old enough to drive, I delivered groceries in their Economy Store van.

My neighborhood may not have been the greatest but I sure thought it was. Here are other staples from my neighborhood from a High Street vantage point:

Fehlinger's Store was on the corner of Parish and Brown. It later became the spot for the new Peters' Economy Store.

Mosie's Confections was on Parrish close to High Street right across from the original Peters Economy Store.

Mosie's eventually became Maria's Pizza. Maria was the wife of Johnny Hyder and the sister-in-law of Bertie Hyder, one of my wife Pat's best friends of today.

Up Parrish Street on the right side was Goode's Dry Goods store. It was right next to Fehlinger's close to Brown Street.

Past Goode's across Brown Street on the corner, was the neighborhood Drug Store which existed back then. Our Drug Store was officially known as Colley's Pharmacy. It was pristine and not only had pharmaceuticals but it also sold fountain pens and great paper.

When we were kids at home we heard youthful accolades in our homes about how good Mr. Goode was. "Mr. Goode is a good man" was a frequent tribute. Karl Goode was a great man.

I got all my clod hoppers from Goode's Dry Goods Store though all us kids in the neighborhood longed for the day that we could wear low cuts shoes.

Goode's was the place before I was old enough to meet my dad at Kranson's store in the Heights, close to The Stegmaier Brewery Company in Wilkes-Barre, where dad worked.

My pants needed replacing often with holes in the knees and I wore out a lot of shoes. Goode's store had it all in our neighborhood.

Later, my barber for life, Bob Amory bought Goode's and he gave haircuts. He was my barber along with my brothers' and my father's.

He was also a great bowler when in my later pre-teen life, I worked as a pin boy and I saw Mr. Amory deliver knockouts to the pins regularly.

Don't Buy Chocolate Milk or Goodies.

Daubert's on Blackman Street, less than a block away was a needed store for many in the neighborhood. They had everything.

My dad had a book with Daubert's and Peters' Economy Store. He paid up every Thursday on his payday.

My family learned from Dad that we could not use the book to buy goodies such as chocolate milk or cupcakes or better lunchmeat like chipped Pullman Ham.

Daubert would write *chocolate milk* in the book and then dad would know.

Mom and Grand Mom said we needed to buy about three or four other needed household items when we got chocolate milk or that delicious chipped Pullman Ham.

When there were too many items for Russell Daubert or Betty Daubert to list on one line of the book, they just put MDSE, for merchandise. Dad never knew that mom or gramma had OK'd the chocolate milk or Pullman Ham.

Maybe he did know because he was so kind—my dad.

Walker's Store was about three blocks from our house. It was on Jones & Brown. and so, we rarely got there. Peters Economy Store was across from the mine shaft on Parrish and High, less than a block away from home.

Albert Peters Sr. was a great man and his sons Thunsie and Butchie and his daughter Emily (angel) in this generation are also wonderful people.

The Peters' family helped all the neighbors and were very kind during the depression and the war. Many could not have survived without the credit and good-will they have received from the Peters' family.

Many have never even to this day been able to repay all they received.

Nick and Mary Nick Solomon had a storefront on their home a half-block from our home. They had lots of bicycles and parts in that store but never sold any. It looked like they might have even have had some electric trains.

The store never opened for business while I was living on High Street.

Irene Solomon, RIP, a recent angel who was also an angel in life, was their daughter and she was my good buddy until she passed away about a year ago. I just loved her as did many in my family as well as George Elias and of course her husband, Ralph and son Ralph and family.

Her married name is Irene Jachimiak and she was married to Ralph. She lived in the first house on Holland Street up from high and across the street from Mike Barrouk's store.

There were always neat things happening in the 'hood. Some were not legal. For example, according to my buddy--George Elias, he knew that Irene's brother, Ace, ran card games out of the basement of Mosie Sallitt's store (after it had closed for good).

He was raided several times by the State Police. That was exciting.

As noted above, while I was growing up, my grandmother would religiously take me up to Goode's store for a brand-new pair of clodhoppers, but not until my old pair had holes in the bottom middle or had lost their soles.

My mother told me that I always used to say: "Mr. Doodie is a dood man." Karl Goode was a good man as were most of the fine men and women in our neighborhood. What a great life. Later on, in life, I was Goode's paper boy.

High Street in Wilkes-Barre was a great neighborhood. A kid with a 26" bike could go anywhere from there.

Chapter 7 Change for a Nickel?

Mike Barrouk, Greg Barrouk's Great Grandfather (Greg is a former Wilkes-Barre City Official), ran a phenomenal candy store on High Street when I was less than five-years-old.

It probably was a much more important store in High Street's earlier days. The picture above is Of Sam's Candy Store with Sam in the picture at his counter. It was a lot like Mike Barrouk's store.

Mr. Barrouk was an endearing man. He had penny candy galore when I was growing up. The many varieties were behind glass counters that only Mr. Barrouk could open.

I had the same dreaming eyes as the kid in this circa 1950 picture of a candy store counter in Chicago.

When I would go into the store, there were always a few Syrian gentlemen there on chairs smoking stinky cigars. I would go in for either candy or change.

Sometimes my family members—typically uncles or aunts from out of town—would ask me as a youngster to go to Mike Barrouk's store to get them some change. I did not ask why.

I still do not know why they did that. Maybe I had to get them cigarettes also.

The store was less than a half block from my house. In this story about Mike Barrouk's store, I was even younger than when Karly Blaine built my first bike.

Two houses separated my house from the candy store. It was great. When I was first permitted to go there, Mike Barrouk always seemed to like it when I came in. I liked him too!

The store always smelled like old cigar smoke with a slight hint of candy confections. If it were not for the candy behind the glass, it would have had little appeal to a kid such as myself.

One day, I figured I needed some change for myself. In fact, what I needed was more change than I had because I knew the more change a kid had, the more things he could buy.

I was beginning to learn about economics and individual supply and demand.

I did not fully comprehend the value of a coin yet because dimes were smaller than nickels yet were worth more.

I knew that, other than that pesky dime, the big coins were always worth more than the little coins.

So, I figured on this particular day, I would put into work my plan of action to get more change into play at Mike Barrouk's "Candy" store.

I went to the counter and Mike Barrouk was there expecting me to ask for candy or change. He was very patient. I asked for change. He said, "What would you like change for?" I had a nickel.

I said, "I would like this nickel changed into a quarter." I knew that if I got the quarter, I could get two dimes and a nickel for the quarter in a subsequent round of change.

Just then, you could hear a pin drop in the store. Other cigar smoking individuals had heard my request.

Mike knew I was too young to be kidding or trying to cheat him, so he asked his friends if they had heard what I said and they all got a good laugh about it.

I was perplexed and did not know why they were laughing. When the laughter died down, Mr. Barrouk took the time to explain the value of coins to me.

He did not get mad or as we say today, "angry." He was a good guy. High Street was a great place to grow up. I left with my nickel still trying to figure it all out. No aunt or uncle had sent me on that "change" mission.

Chapter 8 We Had Two 5 & 10 Cent Stores in Wilkes-Barre

5c & 10c Store like Huntzinger's & Barney St.

There were 5 & 10c stores like Kresge's & Woolworth's & Neisner's in uptown Wilkes-Barre. But, when you were looking for neat things to buy in our neighborhood or close by, Huntzinger's 5 & 10c store was on the list. It was on Hazle Street, about six blocks up Parrish Street hill.

The Barney Street 5 & 10c store was another great place. It was at the other end of High Street down Blackman four blocks, straight across to Horton, down another two blocks on the left side. and it was right next to the Barney Inn on the corner of Barnet and Horton Streets. Both stores were about six blocks from my home.

Huntzinger's was a great store and had all kinds of toys and other things but they did not have bike replacement parts or anything intricate about bikes.

Years after I got my first bike, when I was thirteen, I was hired by Huntzinger's for their stockroom.

When high school football season began that year, I could not make my work schedules at the store and they would not alter the schedule. So, we mutually agreed that I would not work there anymore.

The Barney Street 5 & 10c was well below High Street into South Wilkes-Barre. To get to either Huntzinger's or the Barney Street 5 & 10c, I needed to take my trusty 26" bike.

The walk took way too long. I only walked to the Barney 5 & 10c when the brakes were completely gone on my otherwise trusty 26" bike.

Sometimes to make sure I got the right new bike part, I walked the bike to the store so Leo could look at it.

Today the ole 5 & 10c, without Leo and his pipe in charge, and without a building, has become the parking lot for the Barney Inn on Horton & Barney Streets. It is now known as CrisNics. It is a great place for libations and great food.

For these two stores, as noted, 26" bicycle transportation was absolutely necessary. These venues kept an under ten-year old busy for hours checking out toys, gizmos, sports items, bicycle accessories, and parts.

At the Barney Street 5 & 10c store, the manager smoked a pipe. His name was Leo. I forget his last name.

He seemed to seek me out whenever I arrived. He loved running his 5 & 10c store and he did it well.

He helped me solve foot brake problems with bicycles. He knew how the back rim on bikes worked and he helped me to understand how to take them apart and fix them.

It seems there was this pin in the "New Departure" type back rim that would get bent from slamming on the foot brake. Leo sold the pin for about ten cents. It lasted for months before breaking again.

After I paid for it, with bad brakes, I would often ride home up the hill and then immediately fix my bike. Horton Street hill was steep so I typically pushed the bike up half of the hill.

Leo was why I went to that 5 & 10c store more than Huntzinger's. That one darn part in the "New Departure" brake system kept failing.

Leo made sure he always stocked that part. He was just a good guy. And I was just a kid! His store was right next door to the "Bucket," a neighborhood movie theatre. As I recall, the "Bucket" was also right next to the Barney Inn.

The real name for the Bucket was the Crystal Theatre but I just learned that recently. The parking lot of CrisNic's shown on the right on the next page is where the Crystal Theatre was located.

There was also a movie theatre a block up and across Hazle Street from Huntzinger's 5 & 10c. The Hart Theatre's movies were always more recent and about a nickel more than the Bucket's 15c specials.

With all the places to go in Wilkes-Barre, I always felt that Wilkes-Barre City Father's could not have planned it better—at least for a sub 10-year-old.

Tommy Mehm's Train Set

One day, my buddy Tommy Mehm, RIP, who had an old chicken coop in his yard that we used as a bunk-house, invited me into his home for some serious play time. His mom and dad always fed me though I did not need it.

Tommy was the only boy in his family and it seemed like there were a million female Mehms in the house. They were his mom & sisters and all were nice. By questioning Tommy one day, at our house, my parents found out her maiden name was Larkin.

Mr. Mehm worked for Omalia Laundry and he did well enough to feed them all of them and me too!

Tommy had a Marx Train Set and he liked it but could not make it go. I had some bike making skills at the time and I had become sort of a problem solver. I took a shot at getting the train going.

Tommy asked me to play with his several year older Marx Train set. There was one problem. It had not worked for years.

Whatever prevented us from making it work was simple to fix and we then had hours of fun. We set the tracks up on the rug of Tommy's bedroom on the second floor of the Mehm house on Blackman Street.

Their home was right across the street from St. Boniface School where we both went to school. The Mehms were just so nice. I loved operating that train and so did Tommy. We played for hours at a time.

Chapter 9 How Could a Kid Not Want an Electric Train?

Every Christmas season from when I was about six or seven years old, every Friday night, cold as it might be, I went *uptown* on my trusty 26" bike. By then, it had almost become an appendage.

In most towns, they called central city "downtown." But not in Wilkes-Barre, Pennsylvania, my home town.

Before I got my bike or when it was way too cold, we would take the Grove & Brown Bus uptown, or we would walk to central city for a special movie or special shopping. We said we were going "uptown." Downtown was not a familiar term.

Uptown Wilkes-Barre was a great place to be, especially Public Square. Here is a picture from the late 1950's—early 1960's. Uptown was a beehive of activity.

Uptown Wilkes-Barre was simply magical to visit. From South Main Street to Public Square, it was an eye's delight.

While on my 26" bike, I always stopped at the American Auto Store (the building is now Marquis Art & Frame), to see the Lionel Trains on display.

My buddy Mike Grant's dad managed Murzin's Art Shop for Mose Murzin for 25 years before it was sold to Kenny Marquis. Daniel Grant was as good as it gets in the business.

He then managed it for Kenny Marquis for 13 more years until he passed away in 1983. Helen Novak, a classmate of mine years after this story took place worked for Mr. Grant for years. The years sure go by quickly.

Quite often, while the building was still the American Auto, they were operating the trains on the platforms and the whole place was filled with enchantment.

I cannot find a picture of the old American Auto but, their train displays were as good as factory direct such as the one below:

Look at that huge transformer on the lower right. It was designed to control up to four trains independently. Even Lionel cannot make them anymore.

This transformer had to cost a million dollars compared with my ability to pay for it or any of the platform displayed trains or accessories like you see in the picture. When the trains were running, it was surely impressive.

When I was nine years old riding uptown on my 26" bike, when I stopped, I would tie my bike to a parking meter. I knew there were always bike thieves in the area.

I would get into the American Auto store as soon as I could so I could make it to the counters to see the great Lionel Train displays. Sometimes the store personnel were running the trains which was an extra treat.

The American Auto Store itself was a cut above anything else at the time for Lionel Trains. It used the standard Lionel displays such as the one above and the one on the next page. Impressive!

How could any young boy not want to have something similar but never equal to the magical displays in these pictures.

When I went to the American Auto, their displays were that nice. I always wanted to be by the display that looked a lot like the one in the picture above.

Then, when they decided to run the train special of the day on regular or the Special O-Gauge tracks, I would be there to see it.

Yes, I would wait for others to leave so I could move up to get a better view.

American Auto had several outstanding platforms upon which to gaze and dream. One was on the right side of the store and the other was way in the back.

I made sure I experienced both before I ever left the store.

OK…sometimes I stayed in the store gazing until I was chased. I stayed and watched in amazement.

I loved these miniature electric Lionel trains. There was an auto building right next door where American Auto changed oil, installed batteries, tires, or any part that you bought in the store.

It was a great American store.

When I was sixteen, my dad bought the family a car, and I can recall that we went there, of course, for anything we needed for the car from batteries to tires.

I do not know what happened to the American Auto Stores but for my money, which was little at the time; they were always an American asset for sure.

In my younger days, I have already discussed my little junk route which on Saturdays brought me anywhere from 15c to 40c. It was nice accumulating funds so one day I could buy a train.

I took whatever papers and rags I collected to Solomon's Junk Yard, which was not much more than a block away from my home on High Street.

If I had a lot of rags, which was a real bonanza, I took them to Alexander's. They always seemed to give a better price.

It did not take long for this U-10 junkman to know where to go. To get a train as a nine-year old, I knew I needed to earn more money than the junk route provided.

I saved many of the few dollars I made, but I could never afford a Lionel Train. Lionel was the Cadillac of trains.

At that time in my life at the American Auto as I recall, the least expensive Lionel Train was $14.95 complete and still in the box.

Chapter 10 I Still Love Trains

I guess by now, you have figured out that I have always had a strong affinity towards model trains of all sorts. I still love trains.

I even love the big freight trains from ConRail (left above) and the passenger trains from Amtrak (right above). Conrail today has a line that runs through our neighborhood a few blocks away. It is up on a trestle and goes over the streets.

I do love hearing that whistle several times a day. By the way, as ConRail (US Freight Trains) has gotten more successful, there are many more freight cars on each train.

Sometimes the trains are so long that there are several engines on the front and back. The big Conrail train stops every day for a few minutes at an earthen trestle by the Burger King at West End Boulevard, a few blocks from where I live now. A few railroad personnel get out, walk down the trestle and they bring back a bunch of Burger King's for lunch. How convenient. Then they blow their whistle and they are off.

I even like the big model trains from Lehmann Gross Bahn (LGB). Gross Bahn by the way is German and it means big train.

When I visited Germany in my early twenties, I saw many homes with LGB trains running outside in their front lawns and even in their back yards and gardens. LGB is big in Germany as you would expect.

Inspired by the big outside LGB model trains, after I grew up and we moved, I built a platform 8 feet above our sunroom floor. The train circles the whole 16 X 22 foot room on the ten-inch platform.

That means I have track that goes all around my Sunroom today. The room has a high, cathedral like ceiling with a ten-inch continuous shelf about eight feet up.

My choice of trains for the Sun-Room is a huge Lehman Gross Bahn (LGB) train like the one above circling the whole room from above.

Even Lionel would admit that my Sun-Room upper-deck display of today is a step above Lionel. The tracks look like they are overgrown HO scale.

The dreamer in me is still operative. It says that one day I should put a little automatic door (or perhaps two) in my outside wall, a train switch, a lot of track, and take the train around the outside deck and bring it back through a different miniature automatic door on another side of the Sun-Room.

Thus, it would go from the inside of the sunroom on one side, traverse the whole 70 foot deck outside and then come back with another switch so it could resume circular room operations on the other side.

Right now, this is not a secret plan or an idea but it is a dream of mine and who knows? Sometimes, when I get serious about a dream, it comes true. No great implementation plan ever begins without a great idea and a great design.

Europe Loves Little and Big Trains

When I went to Europe with two friends in the early 1970's, we had purchased a Eurail Pass. (They are still available and are still a deal.)

Our pass cost us $125.00 each in 1974. This gave the three of us unlimited first-class rail travel throughout Europe for three weeks.

We traveled through eight different countries, often sleeping on the train at night to save on hotel expenses.

We were as far north as Copenhagen, Denmark and as far south as Rome, Italy. The trains were erste classe (first class). That is where I saw the outdoor LGB trains in action for the first time.

I recently took an Amtrak train to Myrtle Beach from Philadelphia with a stop off 100 miles out of town in Florence where we rented a car the rest of the way.

I wrote a book about it called *Take the Train to Myrtle Beach*.

On another occasion, I took the Auto Train from Lorton, Virginia to Sanford, Florida. This was another great train experience.

Being a model train buff for so many years, I could not help drift into thoughts about that Amtrak train trip to "Myrtle Beach."

One day I hope passenger train travel in the US will be back as a really first class service for many cities. We need both main line service and a lot of spoke services. .

If the US built the best *high-speed rail system* as implemented in other countries, and it went from Washington, DC to San Francisco, California, a passenger could go cross country in less than eight hours. I say: "Let's do it!"

Chapter 11 Sometimes Dreams Do Come True

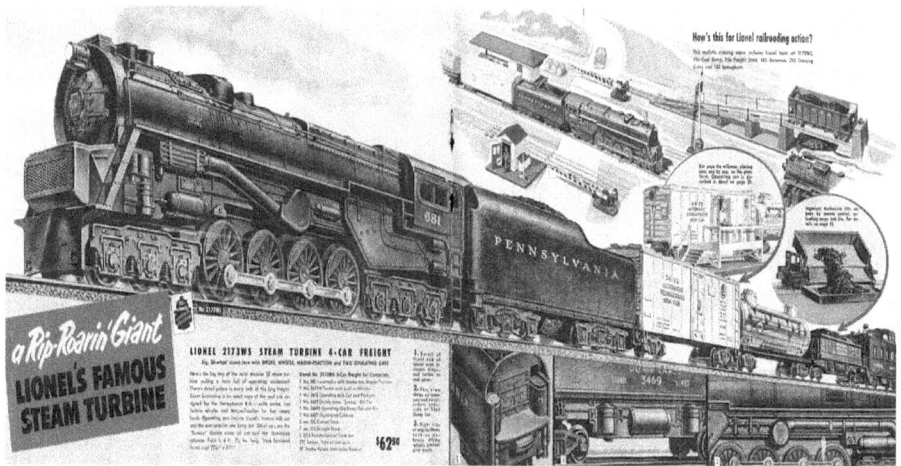

One day, I got my train—the story of a dream fulfilled. It was a Marx Train, not a Lionel or an LGB, but it was a dandy.

Here is that story. It is one of my favorite stories about the goodness of Wilkes-Barre and it is 100% true. I'll be telling about what happened in this chapter and the next.

For me, these were the glory days of my city.

How could a kid—like me—ever achieve a lifetime dream before becoming a teenager?

Where did I get the money?

First of all, on my trip uptown on the last Friday of December 1957, I had more money in my pocket than ever in my life. Secondly, I believe that God wanted me to have a train.

How did I get my huge personal wad of cash? I was industrious for sure, and I worked hard and kept working to collect the wad that I had achieved.

In total, I had $4.62 jammed into my front pocket in a wad when I went uptown to check out what train I could get. I had gotten the bankroll from my normal junk route but I needed more that year to have a shot at a train.

I sold and delivered homemade ice cream cakes for Peters' Ice Cream Store and I had some success doing that.

Also, in November, it had begun to snow in Wilkes-Barre so I tucked some more money away after shoveling some sidewalks. Peters' Ice Cream was my prime location. But, I also had a number of neighbors as customers.

Still I knew that I needed something more this Christmas to have a shot at getting a train. I developed a unique plan for a nine-year old entrepreneur.

To execute the plan, I took my trusty 26" bike up to Huntzinger's store on Hazle Street and I bought some *"stuff"* to use to create something to get that extra pocket money.

The plan was to build something nice that I could then sell to the neighbors.

I bought some red ribbon, some holly beads and some pine cones. With this, some rubber bands and a few bobby pins from my mother's stash, I made several lady's corsages.

The corsages looked pretty nice. In retrospect, I had forgotten a pin for the corsage, but the item was accepted even without the pin.

Unfortunately, I made just one sale, though I had put in a lot of effort and time trying to sell more.

I still remember that Abe Solomon on Parrish Street bought the corsage for his pretty daughter, Reggie. I charged 50c for the corsage. They liked it.

That 50c was enough to pay for every corsage I made—even those I had not sold and I still had a few nickels left over. It could have been a lot worse if I had no sales. Huntzinger's was a reasonable store.

I gave my mom and my older sister Nancy the other corsages as Christmas gifts. I then froze my finances for my last trip uptown before Christmas.

I would not have a penny more than my wad which at the time was $4.62.

Christmas is a great time for electric trains

Every year in December from the time I could mount my "new" 26" bike and leave the neighborhood, I spent a lot of time uptown.

Every Friday night, since there was no school the next day, I visited just about every uptown store in Wilkes-Barre that sold trains.

The last Friday in December in 1957 was December 20. It would be my last pre-Christmas excursion uptown until December 1958.

On this night, when I was almost ten years old, a great thing happened in my life.

It felt like Christmas Eve. I had $4.62 in my pocket from my prior work efforts and good fortune. I was hoping to catch a real bargain on an electric train and I hoped it would be a Lionel.

I got on my 26" bike and I went from High and then down Parrish Street to South Main Street. I took a right onto South Main Street by Mack Brothers' Hardware Store and I was on my way to "Uptown" Wilkes-Barre, PA.

As usual, after riding for blocks on South Main Street, my first stop was on the right in the second block of Central City, Wilkes-Barre. I knew the place as The American Auto. It no longer exists.

There, as always, I got my "wow," from the magnificent exhibition of Lionel Trains on raised platforms. They were on the right side of the store and in the back of the store.

The prices had not gone down and there were no deals. That I admit was a little disappointing. I had never come uptown with such a huge wad ever before.

As usual, the least expensive Lionel Train was $14.99. My $4.62 in my front pocket would probably have to go back in my dresser drawer for another year. At nine years old, I knew for sure this year that Lionel was way out of my price range.

After this unrequited satiation, I browsed a while longer but eventually left the store. My next stop would be "Bushels" of Bargains or just "Bushels" as we called it.

It was in a huge building right next door to The American Auto on the left. I didn't even have to move the bike to check out their toys and trains.

Bushels often had bargains even on trains. But, when I had ever been there in the past, I was not prepared with enough money to buy anything.

I do not remember what I found that night at Bushels but I know that I moved on with no purchase. I loved to see all the train exhibits in various stores in succession. If my bike was willing, so was I.

I got on the 26" bike again and passed Northampton Street on the same side as the

American Auto. This took me to the first block of South Main Street.

The Rea and Derick Drug store was my next stop.

They always had a few trains available that they advertised in the local papers. I read all their ads.

Their ads were very inviting but there was nothing there on this night. So, I went back to the corner and I crossed South Main at the light.

I then stopped at Lazarus' on the opposite side of Rea and Derick. as I did many other times—just in case I might find something. However, the Lazarus Store's toy department was not built to attract older kids like me as I was 9. They had a lot of toys for little boys and girls.

Rarely was there a train but it was worth a look. Little kids liked the Lazarus' store. When I was a little kid, I liked it also!

On this particular night, however, I did have a few bucks in my pocket. I felt a bit different than when I was just window shopping.

Lazarus Store in Columbus, Ohio looks a lot like the Wilkes-Barre store

I had been hoping that I might find something in a store after ruling out American Auto due to my funds insufficiency. I simply could not afford American Auto in 1957.

I left Lazarus' empty-handed but I still had one more place to go.

Eventually I made it to Neisner Brothers further down South Main Street towards Public Square from the Lazarus Department Store.

I still had Woolworths and Kresge's and even Pomeroys Toy Department on the Square to visit, but they never really seemed to have real electric trains though I recall seeing the wind-up variety. Worst case, if there was no chance of anything, I could have stopped at the Boston Candy Kitchen on Public Square or the Spa, down South Main, for a hot chocolate.

In other words, if my Neisner's exploration for trains did not work out, there was the chance I would be key-winding up train engines to go around our tree in 1957. It would not have been that bad and we would be smiling through the entire holiday season, especially Christmas.

In Wilkes-Barre, Neisner's store was right before the Boston Store, Woolworths, and Kresge's. Neisner Brothers' Store was more than a full block up from the American Auto on the opposite side of the street.

Most of us just called this combination 5c & 10c *Department* Store, "Neisner's."

My Aunt Ruth McKeown ran the "Center Fountain" at Neisner's and many times I had a pizza or a soda that Aunt Ruth rang up in the center store fountain register.

Her son Joe, who is about ten years older than me, every year built a magnificent platform with switches and automated milk cars in their wonderful home at 66 Horton Street. I loved seeing Joe operate his great Lionel Train when my dad and mom took us to visit.

It was always great to see Aunt Ruth at Neisner's and the pizza was good too!

Above you can see a picture of the front of the store followed by a pic of the huge side fountain at Neisner's. It was very large. Today we might call it a luncheonette. It had everything in those days.

On my many trips, uptown during December 1957, I had checked out the less expensive trains at Neisner's. I knew their Marx Trains were much less expensive than Lionel.

Yet, I had never checked to see exactly how much it would cost for a full set.

Marx was not as spiffy as Lionel but my buddy Tommy Mehm's train was a Marx and we had a lot of fun with it for years. Tommy's Marx Train had a steam engine pulling the load like the one shown after the Neisner's picture on the next page.

Neisner Brothers store will play a big role in the rest of this story so I am pleased to show another picture of a different Neisner's store bustling with shoppers from many years ago clamoring to get in:

A Bustling Crowd Ready to Shop at a non W-B Neisners

Tommy Mehm-like Marx Coal-Fired Marx Engine

Notice the front and back wheels on the Tommy Mehm engine were not included with this Marx model and the plastic mold was not well formed. But, it worked for Tommy and me and it was great to play with. Nobody had a lot of money in the 1950's.

You can see from the picture that Marx trains of the 1957 era were not exact replicas of real trains as was the Lionel line. But, they were still electric trains and they were still exciting.

I had resigned myself that if I could find any electric train that I could afford, and it was a Marx or American Flier or anything else, I would be happy to bring it home that night. My *bogey* of course was $4.62.

I figured even if I could not get a Marx Train, it was so close to Christmas that I would at least be able to check them out at their lowest prices.

I was getting ready to dream for another year. The total of my wealth was right there in a big wad in my pocket. I knew for sure it would not get me a Lionel Train even if Neisner's had one for sale.

I find it very hard to give up on any idea even if to others it may be just a dream.

Chapter 12 It Felt Different This Time

A handsome wad of cash-- $4.62 or more maybe

I remember that on this night, I felt a little differently about everything. I cannot explain it. I had some hope because I knew that $4.62 in my pocket was not just a buck plus a few dimes.

It was real money and it had taken a lot of time and a lot of effort to earn it.

The constant $14.95 price for Lionel's starter train at American Auto was a big setback for a kid with a wad of dough burning a hole in his pocket. But, as soon as I mounted my 26" special bike to begin my uptown cruise, I knew I would be OK.

Perhaps that night something good would happen, and with $4.62, I was ready just in case it did. But even I, with my glowing anticipating eyes, would never have expected what happened that night.

All the while, my trusty 26" bike was waiting for me just outside of Neisner's store.

When I went into the Neisner Brothers' store on December 20, 1957, I did not even stop at the first-floor Fountain for a coke. I noticed my Aunt Ruth was not on duty and I was not about to spend a dime until I had checked out the trains.

I wanted to have all my funds available. I went right down the steps to where the toys and trains were sold.

It was almost closing time and the basement seemed a little darker than usual. There seemed to be no customers and no sales personnel in the Neisner's basement that night. It was "dead."

I went around to the train displays and I looked longingly as I always did at the boxed Marx trains.

There was enough train showing to make them look almost as glorious as the Lionel's that I had just seen at the American Auto Store.

I was very disappointed to discover that the least expensive Marx boxed model was priced at $8.99. It was lots less than a Lionel but still too much for me.

I had never priced them—more than likely because my big plan was to buy a Lionel one day.

I did have $4.62 so I thought I had a shot at a Marx Train but now even this did not seem like it could possibly happen until at least 1958.

I had bought a lot of trains many times in my dreams but it was pretty obvious that dream was not going to happen for real on this particular night.

I started to think about how I always had dreamed about a train, and yet I still had no train.

It had never happened for real before and I was beginning to get comfortable with the idea that I would have to wait another year or more for this dream to ever come true.

Ready to accept disappointment

Though lots less expensive than the Lionel's, I realized that unless Neisner's had a special model under the counters, I still could not afford any train—even at Neisner's lower prices.

But, I kept browsing, nonetheless. I enjoyed just looking at trains and platform stuff.

I had been disappointed before. So, maybe next year I would save up enough! I had made myself OK with how I figured it was going to end. That's the way it had always been.

Why is the manager coming towards me?

Then, out of the semi darkness of the basement of a department store, a man who looked like he could be the store manager came out of nowhere.

He came right up to me like as if I was why he was there and he asked if he could help me. I had heard "May I help you?" many times from many people and I still had no train. Was he serious?

Most stores did not seem to like a kid hanging around a lot of neat-looking loose toys. I suspected his visit had to do with being concerned that something might be stolen.

Yet, this gentleman looked like he wanted to genuinely help me find what I wanted. He reminded me of Leo at the 5 & 10c. He looked like a regular store guy but he did not act that way He moved around like he was the boss.

I told the man that I was looking for a train but there were none there on display that I could afford.

He did not react to my answer but instead, he simply and gently asked me how much money I had to spend.

I knew I had just $4.62 and that is what I told the man. I expected him to walk away but he did not.

Instead, he looked me in the eyes and he reached down and pulled a huge Marx Train box out from under one of the counters. It already had a load of track in it and a transformer; but nothing else.

It was not really a new train set. It must have been broken up to display certain parts of the set. It was certainly likeable.

Was this man really an angel?

He asked me to come along with him. I was not sure why. He walked around to different areas where they had train cars and parts and platform items.

He got some more track and said that ought to be enough track. He then went about finding Marx Electric Train cars and putting them into slots in the Marx Train box that he held.

Finally, he found a painted diesel shaped engine (not a locomotive like the one with which Tommy Mehm and I played) and he put that into the box.

Everything seemed to fit except *the why*?

Marx gauge M-10005 Union Pacific

Each time he did something like this, he would ask if this were OK or if that were OK. I would say it was OK.

I was not 100 percent sure what he was doing but the dreamer in me thought he just might be building a train set for me.

I knew deep down that I would not be able to afford this fine train as it grew inside the biggest train box that I had ever seen.

And, in case you may not recall, I was sort of an American Auto expert from afar.

He then looked puzzled, asked me to stay where I was, and he started walking briskly from one area to another. Then, he came back to me with a red Pullman (Passenger) train car that looked exactly like the one below

.

He said, "I cannot find a caboose but this car looks an awful lot like a caboose. Will this car be OK for you to use as a caboose?" I said sure. It looked just like the car on the prior page. I am not kidding. I still was not sure what was going on because I had never met an angel before.

He then closed the box and took it to the register. He was also the guy at the register. He had built a whole train set from pieces while walking around the undersides of the basement counters with me.

He sealed the train box so it did not come apart, and then he asked me what I thought of the train that he had built with all of the required parts including a caboose from items found in the store. I told him how much I liked it and he said: "That is great!"

Hard as it is to believe, and I still had not paid for the train set, this man seemed happier than I (I was shocked) that he had put together a unit that I really loved.

You bet I loved it and I loved that a good man like him would even consider doing such a wonderful thing for me or for anybody else in a similar circumstance on the last Friday before

Christmas in the Town of Wilkes-Barre, Pennsylvania. God is good! Is he not?

What a thrilling experience.

I could not contain myself anymore so I then asked him the question of which I dreaded the answer. I asked: "How much is it, sir?" He looked at me like he knew what he had done and he said:

"Why; it is four dollars and sixty-two cents…that's how much you told me you had, right?" I said: "Yes, it is!"

Thank you, sir!

I was crying with joy inside but I showed no tears because my dad always taught me that men do not cry. I spoke again: "Yes, Thank You Sir."

I took out the $4.62 from my pocket. It was in the form of a lot of change and a few bills. I am glad my father was not watching as he always told me cash money should be kept neat with all the faces up. This just looked like a wad.

The man stood there smiling and waiting patiently for me to finish counting and then I handed it all to him.

It was an exact count. He took the wad of money, thanked me for the business, smiled, and he rung up the sale on the cash register. I still could not believe that the Train was mine.

I thanked him again and he said Merry Christmas, and so did I. It sure was a Merry Christmas for me and my family. I could not believe what had just happened. I wanted to hug him. I wish I had.

Wow! What a great life!

I hope he is still alive or his children so they know what a wonderful man there was who once worked for Neisner Brothers Store in Wilkes-Barre PA. It gave me the most positive boost that I had ever received to help me know how great the people of Wilkes-Barre really are.

Thank you, kind sir, from Neisner's in Wilkes-Barre. You represent the overall feeling that I have to say about my city, my town, my hometown, Wilkes-Barre Pennsylvania.

Said differently Wilkesberry, Wilkesberry, My hometown. Thank you, Aunt Bee!

Amen!

Chapter 13 Getting the New Train Set Home to Work

The ride home from Neisner's was exciting

Try finding a picture of a train box on a bicycle handlebar anywhere. I could not and on my way home as a nine-year old, I had no camera to capture this great event so I could show a picture in this chapter. Besides that, it was pitch dark about 8:00 PM on December 20th.

The picture on the prior page was the best online of a bike ready for a big train box that I could find. My bike had no saddle bags like this but I had learned earlier in life how to balance anything on the handlebars and hold it on using my fingers and thumbs or just one hand.

The picture gives you an idea of how hard it would be to balance the train box on the handle bars and also steer the bike.

I was nine years old at the time. In the picture of the bike I found to depict the dilemma, there is no person riding the bike. It is not my bike. It is not dark out. It is not cold and windy out. And, the saddlebag is certainly not the shape of the train box. Yet, I figured with just words and no picture. it would be even more difficult to explain.

But, you can probably imagine what the huge Marx train box would look like on the handlebars of my big 26er without a picture as shown.

Moreover, I had nothing with which to tie the box to the handle bars. I don't think bungee cords were invented yet.

However, I picked this picture because it does give an idea of my trip home from Neisner's store on a cold dark December evening, even though in this picture, the sun appears to be bright in the sky.

My trusty 26" bike was waiting patiently for me outside the Neisner's store. It was cold but I did not feel any cold. I was unexpectedly warm inside after what had just happened.

I rested the huge train box on the handlebars of my 26" bike. I held on to it with fingers and thumbs and occasionally shifted to a one hand carry and I steered the bike with the other hand.

I crossed the street at Northampton and rode the bike back down South Main Street in Wilkes-Barre the full 1.5 miles. I passed Johnny Hakim Circle and I turned left onto Parrish Street. I remember it was very cold. But I was thrilled inside.

I walked it up the big part of Parish Hill, by George Elias's house. The hill never seemed steeper. It was very cold but I still felt warm.

On top of the first Parrish hill, there was a downward slope. I got back on the 26-incher again. The little hill in front of me heading to High Street was nothing and I made it up without a lot of straining.

I made a right onto High Street, and I rode my bike over High Street to our home at the end to 363 High Street right next door to the Mill.

I could not wait to show everybody in the house. I still could not believe what had happened.

All the while that I was riding my bike, or pushing it up Parrish Street, I was dreaming about setting the train tracks up and getting the train running for my mom and dad, grand mom, and my brothers and sisters.

I knew the twins, my little brother Joe and sister Mary would especially like having a train to run. Even my older sister, Nancy and my big brother Edward, would be happy. This train was a first for all of us Kellys.

Our family had never had a train. When I got home, nobody could believe that I had gotten a train for $4.62 so I had to tell them the whole story that I just told you.

Our Christmas tree was already set up in the left corner of the parlor from when you would walk in. Plus, there was a pristine white sheet surrounding the tree at the bottom. It extended for quite an area. As usual, it was beautiful.

The train would look great running on track going around the tree on that beautiful white sheet.

For the dry run, I set up the train track on the living room rug. The pattern of the track formed a huge oval with straight track galore. It was almost as big as the parlor itself or so it seemed.

Tommy Mehm had helped me

I had learned enough about trains from my best St. Boniface School buddy, Tommy Mehm, RIP, from Blackman Street. That's where I got my train experience. Tommy had a Marx Train with similar track.

Yet, at first, with everything set up on the parlor rug, I could not figure out how to connect the transformer to the track. I was so excited about what had happened, I could not think straight.

My dad found some small gauge coated copper wire and it was easy to screw that onto the back of the transformer. But, how to connect the wires to the track was a conundrum. I had forgotten how Tommy and I had done it.

I did not understand how to attach the other end of the thin wires from the transformer to the tracks.

Subsequently, I learned that I could have taped the other end of each of the wires directly to a different rail (outside and middle) of the Marx tracks so they would make contact.

If I could have thought this through or my electrician buddy of today, Dennis Grimes or my electronics whiz, Gerry Rodski could have been whispering directions in my ear, I would have done it more professionally.

The two wires connected to the two outside Marx Train rails by tape would surely have powered the tracks for the train. I just did not know it when I brought the train home on December 20, 1977.

On this night, I was not thinking electricity. So, I concluded that I needed another part that I had seen connected to the tracks at Tommy Mehm's house. It had worked there so what could be different at my house now?

What was that part and what was it called? At first, I could not remember.

Then, I figured it out from recalling Tommy Mehm's train setup. What I was looking for was called a *lock-on*.

I had seen these at the American Auto displays also. All their transformers were connected to the tracks with a *lock-on*. Since a picture is worth a thousand words, here are two pictures of a Lionel O27 lock-on. O27 was very similar if not the same as Marx gauge (sized) track.

To me, the Marx track looked just like the O27 gauge Lionel track. Maybe they were the same. I hoped that a Lionel lock-on for its standard O27 gauge would work for Marx Trains.

If Dennis Grimes were there that night, my personal Mr. Electricity, he would have told me it was a better plan regardless of the track gauge than taping bare wires to the tracks.

I figured the only solution was a *lock-on.* But, how could I get one!!!

I had no money at all. I confessed to my generous grandmother that I needed a part to make the train work. I was nine years old and certainly nine-year-olds never tire. I told her I thought it would not be much more than a dime.

She gave me a quarter and encouraged me to go get one. Everybody in the house wanted the train to work especially if it could work that night.

Without hesitation, and with the quarter in the same pocket that had once held the $4.62, I got on my trusty 26" bike again. It had another mission and it was ready to help me accomplish mine. The American Auto was 1.5 miles from my home.

It was a pitch dark windy cold Friday night. It was getting colder as the night progressed. I worried that the store would be closed. I did not take the time to look at a clock.

I went down high, down Parrish, and then down South Main in the winter cold through the brisk wind and I was soon back at the American Auto Store. It was always well-heated at the American Auto

I knew that Neisner's did not have parts like a *Lock-on*. I had come to believe that American Auto had everything. They did. They were open. The part was fifteen cents.

I have no idea today what time it was. It was magical. It was the last Friday before Christmas. It had to be some time before 9:00 P.M when uptown Wilkes-Barre shut down.

I bought it and came home, all again on this dark, cold, December night with my trusty 26" bike leading the way.

Without the burden of carrying the Marx Train box, the bike got me back home very quickly though the wind was howling into my face.

We had already placed the train on the track. So, I connected the lock-on to a piece of straight track and then connected the wires from the transformer to the lock-on. Doubting Thomas that I was, though logic suggested success, I still was not sure.

Nonetheless it was time. I plugged the power cord of the transformer into the wall. I turned the transformer dial towards run forward.

Everything fit and the train worked for the first time like a charm. Even reverse worked. Everybody in the house was there watching with glistening eyes.

We then disconnected all the track after running the train for a long time. We took just the circular pieces and put them around our beautiful tree on the pristine white sheet.

It all worked and it was like magic when the train went behind the tree and came back out the other side.

It was surely a blessed Christmas for a kid with a dirty face from High Street in Wilkes-Barre, and a family that was in awe of having a train make its trips around their tree.

Marx Seaboard Running Around Christmas Tree

Grand Mom & Grand Pop By the Christmas Tree

These were Wilkes-Barre's glory days for sure. Thinking back, I wish I had taken notice to the name of the man who helped me get a train for $4.62.

I often thought I should have written him a letter because of how good he made me feel as well as my whole family. It was a miracle. I hope God gave him many Merry Christmas' with his family.

Now it is my turn to give something back. It is now my turn to hang around some downtown Wilkes-Barre stores looking for some dirty-faced kids like me. I'd love to help them get their first train. Maybe as you get older, you too can do the same.

Lots of smiles sure come with a nice train set, whether it is Marx, American Flyer, HO, Lionel, or LGB. Thanks for letting me tell you this story.

Isn't it nice to know such great people still exist in this world? At this time in my past life, my whole world was in Wilkes-Barre, PA. And Wilkes-Barre always delivered the best.

Merry Christmas to all and to all a good night! May your good dreams be reality and your bad dreams never be more than a thought gone awry. Enjoy your whole life vigorously and don't ever discount yourself. You can do anything.

Life, especially during the magical season of the Lord, Christmas, is wonderful for sure.

Merry Christmas

Other books by Brian Kelly: (amazon.com, and Kindle)

Please take a run out to amazon.com/author/brianwkelly when you have time to find another book by Brian Kelly that you might enjoy.

The Bill of Rights By Founder James Madison Refresh *your knowledge of the specific rights granted to all*
Great Players in Army Football Great Army Football played by great players..
Great Coaches in Army Football Army's coaches are all great.
Great Moments in Army Football Army Football at its best.
Great Moments in Florida Gators Football Gators Football from the start. This is the book.
Great Moments in Clemson Football CU Football at its best. This is the book.
Great Moments in Florida Gators Football Gators Football from the start. This is the book.
The **Constitution Companion.** A Guide to Reading and Comprehending the Constitution
The Constitution by Hamilton, Jefferson, & Madison – Big type and in English
PATERNO: The Dark Days After Win # 409. Sky began to fall within days of win # 409.
JoePa 409 Victories: Say No More! Winningest Division I-A football coach ever
American College Football: The Beginning From before day one football was played.
Great Coaches in Alabama Football Challenging the coaches of every other program!
Great Coaches in Penn State Football the Best Coaches in PSU's football program
Great Players in Penn State Football The best players in PSU's football program
Great Players in Notre Dame Football The best players in ND's football program
Great Coaches in Notre Dame Football The best coaches in any football program
Great Players in Alabama Football from Quarterbacks to offensive Linemen Greats!
Great Moments in Alabama Football AU Football from the start. This is the book.
Great Moments in Penn State Football PSU Football, start--games, coaches, players,
Great Moments in Notre Dame Football ND Football, start, games, coaches, players
Cross Country With the Parents A great trip from East Coast to West with the kids
Seniors, Social Security & the Minimum Wage. Things seniors need to know.
How to Write Your First Book and Publish It with CreateSpace
The US Immigration Fix--It's all in here. Finally, an answer.
I had a Dream IBM Could be #1 Again The title is self-explanatory
WineDiets.Com Presents The Wine Diet Learn how to lose weight while having fun.
Wilkes-Barre, PA; Return to Glory Wilkes-Barre City's return to glory
Geoffrey Parsons' Epoch... The Land of Fair Play Better than the original.
The Bill of Rights 4 Dummmies! This is the best book to learn about your rights.
Sol Bloom's Epoch ...Story of the Constitution The best book to learn the Constitution
America 4 Dummmies! All Americans should read to learn about this great country.
The Electoral College 4 Dummmies! How does it really work?
The All-Everything Machine Story about IBM's finest computer server.

Brian has written 131 books in total. Others can be found at amazon.com/author/brianwkelly

www.ingramcontent.com/pod-product-compliance
Lightning Source LLC
LaVergne TN
LVHW051841080426
835512LV00018B/2997